PATTERNS IN LIFE

Mary Ann Costantini

Noble House
Baltimore, Maryland

Patterns in Life

Library of Congress
Cataloging in Publication Data
ISBN 1-56167-612-8

Library of Congress Card Catalog Number:
00-102665

Published by

8019 Belair Road, Suite 10
Baltimore, Maryland 21236

Manufactured in the United States of America

To my family, who have encouraged, supported, and strengthened me. Without their love, understanding, and patience, this book would have remained only a distant dream.

Contents

Nature Ain't Neat

There'll never be colors straight and true
Like red and green and yellow and blue.
Nature has painted a special treat
For us to see that nature ain't neat.
The sea she tints with a turquoise sheen,
With ebony, silver, and coral.
Conflicting hues shall never be seen
In amber, cadmium, and royal.
Regal mounts of amethyst, azure,
Sienna, with specks of vert, pictured sure.
Floral patterns dot the varied schemes;
Nothing sure is ever what it seems.
She splashes the sky with sapphire and gray;
Current weather plainly does she say.
Wisps of white will evermore repeat
The simple fact that Nature ain't neat.

A Deafening Sound

Heavy dark stillness
Surrounding precious life is
A deafening sound.

Weeping Willow

The weeping willow
Reaches out in its sorrow
To bring life's beauty.

Pictures

Our memory turns
Still-framed pictures to movies
With little effort.

Transformation

The shadows bend in silent streams,
As water flows, refracting light.
The world appears in different beams;
Its shapes and hues hold awesome might.

There are no straight and lofty trees.
Deliberate and sturdy bends
Transform each one of all of these;
Time's age and secret growth ascends.

The gentle breeze and waters flow
For all things' honor, grace, and peace.
A change occurs that's sure and slow,
But knowledge and growth will increase.

Seldom straight is transformation,
All so true in God's creation.

Guardian Angel

Forever you are by our side
While we trod through life's passage each day
Protecting as we walk or ride,
Gently guiding what we do and say.

You give us comfort and support,
Sweet Guardian, companion, and friend
God's will you carefully report
And the wicked fight unto the end.

Our needs and prayers you gently take
To our Heavenly Father above.
Your charges here you ne'er forsake;
Gracing us with God's Heavenly love.

Abundant Noise

In the vast silence
    noise in abundance
    is clearer than I
    could have ever thought
    was possible in
    this world where I live.

The shadows dance to
    silent music as
    if deafening drums
    call out existing
    mankind's humanness.

My Paper

This paper I have on my knees
Was carefully made out of trees.
It's scrawled with black ink.
So what could I think
When it flew away with the breeze?

Alpha and Omega

The Alpha and the
Omega is a silent
Mystery untold.

Lessons

Within the confines
Of experiences, lessons
Are knowledge branches.

Cold Winds

Ice cold winds shall blow, my friend,
In the night as well as day.
Sooner, later, they do end;
Not until nature shall say.

All seasons know its coolness;
Both the wise and shallow know.
Breezes may have gentleness,
Yet, fury may also show.

The mood may be quite pronounced,
Taking different length to die.
Wind's favor praised or denounced,
But it's said with you and I.

Weather Changes

Pressures rise and fall
As weather changes faces,
Changing sun for rain.

Looking Deep

If I look down deep
Inside I will find a few
Unknown surprises.

Motivation

Even the vast sea cannot
Transform without
Something motivating.

Effects of a Stone

Into the pond I cast a stone;
The effects reach to parts unknown.
In time, peace restores glass surface
While change takes place beneath its brace.

What is added, no one will see,
Irritant settles in to be.
Life will soon accept and adapt;
Waters engulf in case-like wrap.

Gull

He soars on in search of food,
Up and down the coast, out and in.
He walks on sand, and later floats
On the sea in hopes to view
Something delicious floating by.
Fish or crackers by human hand,
He finds nourishment enough,
To satisfy partial hunger,
As well as some salt and some sand.

Memories

Without warning, the scene plays,
Acting and reacting in full view,
Touching deep the soul's night and days
In both the past and the new.

Forward comes the memory
With colors of ancient hue.
Dreams awake in reverie;
Consciousness fades the true.

My Mother

I know this Lady
Who taxis, cooks, and cleans,
Lives to serve others,
And follows her faith.
Encouragement and
Trusting compassion
She extends in
Her own special way.

I know this Lady
Who cherishes the
Family's memories
She stores in her heart.
She always guides us,
Embracing us with
Care, never showing
Her anger or her fears.

I know this Lady
Who helps those in need,
Giving of herself
Until there's no more.
Through a hidden voice
Of steady concern
I hear concealed tears
Of sorrow and joy.

I know this Lady
Who has given life,
All she possesses,
And her loving faith.
She's fed the hungry,
Helped the poor and sick.
I know and love her;
She is my mother.

Change of Seasons

In winter, spring, summer, and fall,
He plays different games with a ball.
He'll run and he'll kick
He'll bounce and he'll click;
Then he'll yell just to disrupt it all.

Minor Miracles

In the midst of mist
Minor miracles make the
Hazed memories clear.

Hearing Freedom

Freedom rings for all
To hear if only careful
Attention exists.

War Torn

War torn, I end another day
I go to sleep bandaged in hope.
Morning will come in full array;
I ask courage and strength to cope.

In my ears ring explosions full;
My sight holds its visions unkind.
Tension on my body does pull,
Creating fears within my mind.

Our foes close in to block our way;
This land I have sworn to defend.
Hold fast we must, we shall not sway,
On each other we all depend.

Today I saw my best friend die.
Beliefs and love he shared with mine.
No one there saw me turn to cry.
We'll meet again another time.

Popularity

Popularity,
Is not always itself,
Sought nor popular.

Happiness

Happiness is as
Individual as each
Life seeker involved.

Unconditional Love

Unconditional love
Contains both its own
Happiness and sorrow.

Diamond's Distortion

Misty
translucent
white puffed vapors are
forming their configurations in
the air, from expelled breath, as I walk
on an unusually frigid winter's morning. They
create varied distortions, adding their
own contribution to the flawless
diamonds present in the
descending
snow.

Nature, Time, and Life

Mother Nature and old Father Time,
Knowing forever, still in their prime.
Beauty shows as in the art of mime;
Life's problems are not without their rhyme.

Animal kingdom and human race,
Can read the life upon every face.
Throughout all errors, feel no disgrace;
It's a part of life we all embrace.

Each lesson taught, I must learn it well.
Its use once again, no one can tell.
I use all senses from sight to smell;
Each a precious moment no one can sell.

I need take heed, life's implication;
Two-foot or four, we're in relation.
Only mind sees humiliation,
Each day of life contains vacation.

Time and nature has everything planned;
Each moment in life's a grain of sand.
Rise up together to take life's stand.
Animal kinship abounds with man.

Like a Child

If each of us could only be
As happy as a child,
We would be unbound and carefree,
Seldom tense or beguiled.

The clear blue of the sky above
Would be as black and white;
The mystery of the world of love
Would be as pure as light.

The solid earth beneath our feet
Would help us move along.
Our games would bring us small defeats
To help us to grow strong.

Fantasies would be free and wild;
And colorful, vast interests
Would be simple and mild,
Continuing until our rests.

The Mystery

They were called one day to leave their time
To journey to another place and time.
They packed their things and got on that plane.
To their surprise, it took them Homeward again.

They left their things and their love behind.
Their story is untold and their own is blind
As to details of who and where and how and why.
This great mystery will be held until after I die.

Maybe someday we'll be one in His peace.
The mystery and questions will no doubt cease.
That understanding and love once more will reign,
For us united at Home once again.

Proud Standard

Fluttering in the breeze
The proud colorful standard
Shows its majesty.

Currents

Currents rage beneath
The stillness of liquid glass
Of the vast deep sea.

Beliefs

It is not choosing
Your beliefs that's difficult,
But living by them.

Bounty

The bounty of the world we know;
All others seen will live and grow.
In poverty and wealth alike
Still reaches out enough to strike.
If all take heed from nature's plan;
We'll live and die in beauty's span.
Fruitfulness will ripen for everyone to see
The bounty for us all, each person be.

What Is Love?

Love, what is it?
What does it do?
Is it part of life?
Does it have an accurate definition?
Does it have limitations?
Where do you find it?
What does it cost?
What exactly is love?
To whom does it appear?
Is love freely expressed,
or is it banned?
Can love be visible,
or is love blind?
Do you keep it to yourself
or share it?
Is it sporadic or planned?
Is love a fake,
or is it really real?
Can we possess it;
can we use it,
or give it away?
Does it possess
or is it possessed?
How can it be known?
What are its signs and shapes?
If I could only be sure.

The River

Carrying its life along
the river flows.
It gathers material,
both old and new,
Disregarding obstacles
as on it goes.

Time and Memories

The time shall forget
But buried deep, memories
Shall always remind.

Road Maps

Often road maps do
Not provide grace periods
For unseen road curves.

My Father

The giant standing next to me
Is someone I hold dear.
Protecting, seeing oh so clear
In all that's far and near.

His big frame towers, reigns supreme
O'er all in stream and field,
Not wavering amid life's stream,
His sword of kindness wield.

Standing firm in all his beliefs,
Truth, honor, as his code,
He gently guides for my relief
And lifts my childhood load.

Snowflakes

The soft snow falls like scattered seed;
Hope and beauty are planted here
Supplying a relief from greed
And spreading a blanket of cheer.
Unique are the crystallized flakes;
A delicate lace pattern screens,
Refracting rainbows that it makes,
As best as it can with its means.

The Turkey

There once was a little turkey
Who awoke one day feeling perky
'Til he heard the man
With an axe in his hand
Say, "Now I can have some jerky."

Oversight

In eagerness to find
The answers, the obvious
Has been overlooked.

Uneven Symmetry

Random uneven
Symmetry holds a special
Beauty all its own.

A Stranger

I saw different people and strange sites;
The time was different, the days and nights.
For I was a stranger in a strange land,
But I found a friend, and a helping hand.

My main problem was communication;
To know their tongue would help the situation.
I guess an action speaks louder than a word,
Because, it seemed as if they'd really heard.

He does things different, and yet the same.
For, even though I did not know his name,
He somehow became a very good friend,
And I'll remember him until time ends.

Beware the Darkness

Beware the darkness that blindness brings;
With fear in hearts, no joyous song sings.
The temperatures rise and the heart pounds,
The sound of throbbing pressure resounds.
Look at the forest and miss the trees.
A day will come for each one to see.

Sincere Prayer

The strongest influence
in our lives cannot
compare to sincere prayer.

Crossing the River

By the waters of this deep river,
A lecture did my "Prof" deliver.
He said, "If you knew
What makes the sky blue,
Then you'd know how to cross the river."

Joyous Light

There is no match to
The joyous light that shines from
The eyes of a child.

New Light

Within the sheltered light of dawn
A new day does unfold in birth.
The new has come, the old has gone
For new creation on the earth.

Extending arms embrace the light
That shines upon the infant face.
In time will come the dark of night;
Before that shall come thought and grace.

Experiences tell the tale
Of life lived well and knowledge gain.
Full color shown that shall not pale;
The fleeting stars shall not remain.

The brightness then shall show the way
When born shall be a brand new day.

Betrayed

How could this fate have been?
This love of mine has strayed.
Loss has replaced the win,
For I have been betrayed.

The closeness that we felt
Has turned blood red from heat.
A black hand I've been dealt;
A slow but sure defeat.

I did not see it come
This test of loyalty.
It has left me numb
In cold reality.

The Game

They say it's how you play the game
Not if you win or lose;
But what transpires is simply put:
It's all in what I choose.

Black or white is what is stated,
Or done, as I may see,
But gray creeps in without a word;
Its presence ever be.

Each condition falls into place
And roams about carefree.
But not without the pro and con,
Which will forever be.

Vacation Reminiscence

Into the fire I set my gaze;
The embers spark my memory.
My mind flows back to bygone days
Contented times so full and free.

This cabin held our summer rest
Our laughter flowed, along the lake
We swam or walked, and tried our best
For new bonds together to make.

We kept the simple life in stride;
Each member we enjoyed as one.
Forgetting speech we held our pride
From dawn until the day was done.

Vacation time made cloth of dreams;
And memories had sewn the seams.

Little Flo

A baby fur ball joined my family.
She had sad eyes, yet was happy.
Her little tail wagged constantly;
She always showed curiosity.

The little babe's eyes reflected the light;
My little fur-ball's so cute and bright.
As babes do, she sleeps day and night;
But when awake nothing's out of sight.

When full grown, she'll be very tall;
She's just so ornery and small!
Four little feet, floppy ears, and all,
Colored light and dark, my little fur-ball.

Her love to show, she constantly tried;
As I recall, she never cried.
Our fur-ball baby, we did decide
To name Little Flo until she died.

An Astronomer

An Astronomer that I once knew
Tried to tell me what's old and what's new.
He pulled out a chart.
When I did depart,
He yelled, "Science just isn't for you."

Privilege of Rank

The privilege of
Rank coincides with duty
And priority.

Destiny

Destiny, for all of us, is just right down the road.
When we aid another, it helps lighten our load,
The hand of fate can smile on us, each and every one.
It's cool or warm, light or dark, when our day is done.

Saving a kitten from life's forest branch,
Diving from the safety of that thing called chance,
Wrapping in warmth from a blanket of new fallen snow,
Are only a few ways to help a friendship grow.

People meet in daily routine, passing without a word.
Their actions seem as if only the walls have heard.
Down the road, they labor hard for turning the other way.
Possessions fall into place, yet contentment doesn't stay.

Walls come alive and listen to the language there;
Forest dark and wild flowers blossom into stair.
Each turn in the path that life constructs and start to
begin—
Contests and races each one of us can win.

Which path brings to us the kitten and the snow?
The oak tree doesn't bend at all; it's not that far to go.
Catch the fallen star, and the kitten doesn't fuss.
The hand of fate brings our destiny forth straight to us.

My Heart and Pen

My heart and pen, sometimes write on and on;
The time is here, and then it's gone.
Sometimes I just sit down and write,
It's rare what's read is mostly right.
Sometimes I don't know what to say,
It just comes out in it's own way.
When I reread the words put down
I'll simply smile, or cry, or frown.
But there are times when I'm amazed
At the outcome of my blind craze.
It's seldom prefect every time,
And often there is no set rhyme.
For what I wrote, each little part,
Has come directly from the heart.

Beneath the Snow

Beneath the blanket
Of new fallen snow lies a
Life beyond compare.

Identity

Much can be removed
in life except the
soul's identity.

Night's Light

In the darkness of
The uncertain night, the calm
Silent faith is light.

Good Night

Good night, my little darling child.
The Sandman's come to take your hand,
Like all the children sweet and mild,
Into the wonders of dream land.

There are so many pleasures here
For all the children to enjoy.
A special one is for you, dear;
He's even brought your fav'rite toy.

May you slumber in sweet peace
My little one, my gentle love.
I pray your worries and fears cease,
And that God bless you from above.

I'll see you in the morning's light.
Sweet dreams, my darling, and good night.

The Rock

Upon the Rock, I place my life
For all's not what it seems.
Without the joy and pain in life,
There can't be growth or dreams.

The swaying bend of each tree there
Brings challenges anew.
Engulfed within the sea of care,
The Rock stands firm and true.

Coexisting Conditions

The coexisting
Conditions are not without
Generous merit.

Young Lizzie

Young Lizzie was very dizzy;
She ran around in a tizzy.
She went to and fro
But she didn't know
It's all right not to be busy.

Chosen Lost

None is lost save that
Which is chosen to fade
To oblivion.

The Sea

Constant motion's the path it takes each day
Never ending, repeating, or slowing,
Never lose or gain; nothing in it's way.
Part of it dies, yet some is still growing.

Its sense of nature builds, yet will destroy.
Man does not know it's total mysteries,
But respects too much to use as a toy.
Does it house future or past histories?

Who knows the mighty source of power and life?
Who could ever extend the imagination
Of it's reefs, and caves, and tunnels, and life?
Who can understand the mystery of creation?

The calm, fury, danger, serenity!
This thing of beauty, wondrous thing of love
Is not in space; 'tis our own precious sea.
May we be one both below and above.

Abundant Joy

Clearer rain could not
Fall than the abundant joy
That surrounds our hearts.

My Future

I cannot turn around
Without thinking what future
My life has in store.

Change

Unless change is a
Conscious acquired result,
It will not occur.

Far Away Toys

Through the bars I peer
To all that I hold dear,
For what I want I fear
Is far away, not near.

Mom and Dad will come
When my nap is done.
I'm sure they'll give me one
My battle will be won.

Still Waters

Still waters can run fast and deep.
A wall can begin to thicken.
My life becomes complex and steep;
My pace then can slow or quicken.

It's up to me with my mistakes,
To learn, or to tighten the rack.
My trust and growth is all it takes
To face life or to turn my back.

Deep in my mind, my thoughts run deep;
The currents are still or flowing.
In life given, I laugh, I weep;
Whichever, I keep on growing.

What takes its toll on me is time,
In my life, the weather changing.
Each second is yours and is mine,
We are simply rearranging.

I trip and fall, and then I stand;
The water level seems to rise.
Is rushing past what we demand?
Or is the deepness in surprise?

Dimes Spent

In her youth, she had squandered each dime.
If she just had a nickel each time,
Then she would be rich.
She got that old itch
Just to spend it without thought or time.

Nets

Nets may prevent falls
But they may also construct
Patterned bonds of walls.

Opposites Meet

Steam rises from the
Cup by the sill, while clouds grow
On the frosted pane.

Thoughts of You

I have been thinking about you
      But God only knows why.
Something down deep inside has brought
      You to my mind's surface.
Shadows of vivid memories
      bring forth times long past
When we were friends, the happy times,
      Before fate dealt it's blow.

We danced and laughed; we played our part
      on life's expansive stage.
The feeling deep within our heart
      Could not hold the blank page.
Twelve years have passed without a word
      But not without a thought.
Visions and prayers said silently
      Have brought me no answers.
I pray you are alive and well
      For, that's all I can do.
May God provide you protection
      And happiness in life.

Waiting

Waiting, waiting for just the right moment
To say something, or for the phone to ring,
Or for many other such instances
That should be, but yet, are not happening.
Why is it so much a part of our lives?
Why does that thing called anticipation
Turn into want, need, or hesitation?
Why can we not fill that voided section
Of our lives with something that is worthwhile?
If we use given gifts that are such a part
Of our being, would we then have more
To fill those gaps, and be less hesitant?

The Lift

The weight upon my shoulders has
been lifted. I no longer feel
as if my life is lived below
in the sub-basement of a
tall building that is centered in this
metropolis. My prayers have been
answered. I have been provided with a
lift. I ascend again. Each stop
through unclosed doors I see light through
a window opposite my car.
To my surprise, the doors close and
I am taken higher. I get
off at the last stop, able to
breathe clean air again. Though the door
is overhead, my way is now
bearable since I am lighter.
I possess new found freedom.

Birth of Dawn

Dawn appears,
gently prodding through
the black void,
Its light
slowly diffusing the
realm of darkness.
Hope,
its new life,
is born.

The Cat

The cunning creature stalks they say
For sport, play, food, or fun.
In time, the laziness shall stay
Not energy to run.

The feline is independent
As humankind shall see;
Of keepers, they are confident
Giving them company.

The keepers give free food and care,
But on their way they go
To look through pane, seeming to stare,
While resting on pillow.

Contentment seems to be their own
From playful kitten, through
Until they are completely grown;
Loved friend of me and you.

No Change

If quarters, and nickels, and dimes
Could have their own reasons and rhymes,
They would never jump,
Just stay in the slump.
Inflation would only be mimes.

Free Gifts

Free gifts are given
out of love. All we have to
do is accept them.

Life

Within each person,
Life does not always commence
At the beginning.

Marine Call

Rising up while dark in the morning,
We get ready and start our day.
Marching alive before new dawning,
Once again, we are on our way.

Discipline is in our being;
Strong loyalty uniting us all well.
We're learning each day, always seeking;
A true Marine life, one can tell.

Dedication that knows no bounds
We're in service to our great land.
All in one voice, an echo resounds
Raising the Colors for our land.

Courage and honor, we try to show
Each one's respect, we won't ignore.
If conflict comes, we will march and know
"First to Fight" is our Marine Corps.

We'd rather have peace instead of fight;
We'd rather say to all we care.
If duty calls, we go day or night.
Our jobs we'll do; we will be there!

Resurrection

Sometimes,
under the guise
of ideas
of "Cause" or "Justice"
the truth is hidden.
It is buried
deep
under the rich,
black soil
as put
to rest in
a casket.
Resurrection
will come.

The rinsing from
erosion
will remove
layers,
uncovering
the box
whose lid
will not be
able to
restrict its
occupant.
Truth will
shine for all
to recognize.

Power of Love

The strength of love will always be
A bright old kind of mystery.
It brings new birth in each one here
Holding all close, and very dear.

No definite terms does it hold.
For male and female, young and old.
If truth be told, each one will see
What is meant for you and for me.

Breathing Goodness

To breathe goodness
Brings pureness to body and the
Spirit of the soul.

The Wise Owl

The wise owl reserves
Judgment by not fact, but
Rather asking, "Who?"

Magic

Magic embraces
The atmosphere when one heart
Joins its companion.

Span of Time

Within the span of limitless time
The mind can never truly rest.
Within the span of each one's life rhyme
Completion is subject to test.
If knowledge and wisdom could be owned
By all upon this hallowed earth,
The sunsets would turn to sunrises;
The cessation would turn to birth.

There are so many misconceptions,
Great misunderstanding roams free.
Too many of human's perceptions
Bind tightly that which should be free.
Sighted turns blind, and hearing, deaf,
And speech is muted, but yet
Try though we may some walls aren't destroyed,
Because our pain cannot forget.

With the help of God, a few succeed
Brick by brick the walls topple down.
Light begins to shine with strength restored;
The warmth of life's echoes resound.
What of muted voice that's not heard?
Fragments have remained closed inside,
For the time is not right now, of course,
The joy and pain in them reside.

In this sea, beauty and life are found
If only we will choose to see.
In darkness' depth predator hide,
But in their schools they will not be.
The cleansing waves will wash out the pain,
And rid the sand from the blind's eye.
A clearer hope and vision remain
Broken walls view bright sapphire sky.

The Tug

Where are you going
up the calm river
with loaded cargo
to be delivered?

Your pathway is set
on waters of glass;
each loud toot is heard
from high polished brass.

Service Past

My time of serving is finished.
I was proud to fight for our land.
The hard times have not diminished
The given right to take a stand.

I raised our colors bold and true,
I buried friends amid the fight.
If not clad in our green and blue
My life's way would not have been right.

This injury that I've sustained
Has stripped away that part of me;
In my heart, service has remained;
That way of life brought life to me.

I sit now and watch others go;
Life can't be lived again, I know.

Growing

Growing is a vital part
Of life's eternal quest.
From birth where we made our start
Through old age, worst and best.
Going through each lesson there,
We fell and scraped our knees,
Or climbed each step on the stair,
Or soared above the trees.

Pvt. Pig

I watched my comrade, Pvt. Pig.
Holes back and forth did he dig.
For he didn't learn
To take his own turn
Without comments loud and big.

Opposites

Opposites only
Serve to enhance the strength of
United contrast.

Moon and Mother

The moon shines its light
On all, as mother's love rains
Upon her children.

New Strength

In the darkness of the still night
We can roam about without end.
Settled feelings cannot seem right;
Onward search, time enough to spend.

During the bright light of the day
The quest continues on once more.
There are no words for me to say
But the questions of life still pour.

Beaten down, I will rise to fight
With all strength in body and mind.
Reasons to live bring on new might
Survival again I will find.

Many come to be by the side
Of right and just, hope it will give.
Questions' answers within reside,
The new strength gives courage to live.

Judgment

Our judgment can be
Described as hesitation
With reservation.

Blessed Are the Hills

Blessed are the hills
That witness the birth of dreams
And the richness of life.

Strength

What awesome strength lies
Beneath the surface of the
Sea's firm convictions.

Creativity

Creativity knows no bounds
When imagination is there.
Ideas take on solid form
By all the senses we possess.
Ever part of the creator,
Shall be transformed to viewer's mind.

What Can You Do?

What can you do but try and pray
To put up with what others say
Behind your back in a strange way?
What can you do but try and pray?

What can you do to get along
When it feels that you don't belong?
Do you play the game or just be strong?
What can you do to get along?

What can you do when things aren't right?
They start to improve, but dulls the light;
A cloud appears that blocks the sight.
What can you do when things aren't right?

What can you do when you're put down?
You try to speak, but there's no sound
Because the echoes do resound.
What can you do when you're put down?

What can you do to keep the peace?
When arguments break out, not cease?
Tasks aren't hard, yet, do increase.
What can you do to keep the peace?

Bob Bobber

Bob Bobber had bought a balloon
That bounced from a babbling baboon.
But Bob soon got bored
And bought the whole board,
But baffled Bob bounced to the moon.

Freedom's Flight

Aloft is the winged
Soul that claims freedom's flight through
The purest clear sky.

To My Love

Just what can I say
To the man that I love
Sharing night and day
And God's gift from above?

I thank you for you
Everything that you are
And all that you do;
You are my shining star.

I'm glad that you're mine,
And Dad to our children;
A gift for all time
My own gift from Heaven.

Autumn View

You are so beautiful this time of year
With reds and gold, and purples, green and brown.
Each holding shades forming pictures so clear;
Too soon your radiance will trickle down.
Auburn is sprinkled with verde and or,
With rust and crimson droplets joining in.
There are no new crops left in nature's store,
So I must wait for spring's life to begin.

The Hawk

The hawk flies free and soars on high
When he's unhooded and set free.
But even so sees partial sky
Returning out of loyalty.

The caretaker he loves so dear
Whose patience calmed the wild will.
Mutual respect shows clear
For freedom's strength holds ever still.

During flight he scans the view.
The hunter spies on low terrain
While watching over old and new,
The prey that tries to run again.

And with feast done, he's homeward bound;
His cries of triumph do resound.

Bond of Friendship

It is said that pure love through all knows no bounds.
A friendship united; an echo resounds.
Caring and sharing play only a small part;
Honesty and care come direct from the heart.

Confrontations and problems are put aside
When the trials of another in them reside.
For to lend and ear, is just a trifle aid
To lighten the burden that problems have made.

Bond of friendships grow each day, strengthened by love;
Together, heartaches are lightened from above.
No burden's too heavy, nor gladness too light
That a firm loving friendship cannot make right.

Together through gentle tears of joy or sorrow,
Created friendship gives space enough to grow.
The special bond strengthens, standing firm and tall.
This friendship united, will withstand it all.

Jellyfish

Jellyfish do not laugh, cry, or sing;
Nonchalantly they reach out to sting.
Crafty and sly?
I wish that I
Thought a suit of armor to bring.

Colors

The colors of this world
cannot be described as
pure, but as mixture.

Raise the Standard

Raise the standard bold and high
To show freedom's won colors true.
Battles won from mountain high
To the seas of clear wondrous blue.

The red of blood that was shed,
The white of light and purity,
The sky blue above our head,
Together for our pride to see.

Strike the band for tunes to rise;
Let each patriot's song ring clear.
Let it be then no surprise
What we hold in our hearts so dear.

Gentleness of Touch

Gentleness of touch
Bears peace and serenity
To the mind and soul.

Parallel Lines

Parallel lines are
Met as lives pass in daily
Blind and deaf routine.

Bad and Good

Because of the bad
The goodness has become more
Pronounced and defined.

Done Through Fog

Smoke fills the room;
Fog covers the bay.
Nothing seems too visible
Within the light of day.

Growth is then stumped;
Thoughts arise in each mind.
The workdays fill the time
Within each of his kind.

Nightfall seems quick
For nothing was done;
The challenges of the day
Brings the proof that I've won.

Sunset's Peace

In sunset's peace we watch the dark
    Approach while we reminisce
On joys of our fulfilled days, yet
    Each trial was sealed with your sweet kiss.

In childhood and youth we learned
    The lessons taught by joy and pain.
Too many bridges have been burned
    But sturdier ones still remain.

We've worked and played, we've laughed and cried;
    Our life has been well worth it all.
In giving love, we both have tried
    To build the peace, destroy the walls.

The day has past, it's time to rest
    We'll sleep tonight; we've done our best.

Kiss

The breeze kisses the
Leaves as trees gently bend in
Fanning the wind's love.

Philosophy

Philosophy is
just a state of convictions
held fast with belief.

Contemplation

Contemplation can
Be one of the most useful
Tools we can posses.

Think Again

The bosses that I had at work
Sometimes thought of me as a jerk.
They did not understand
Their little spot of land
Was bought by 'lil' me gone berserk

Deciding

By deciding not
To be judgmental, we have
Decided our case.

The Horse

Running free and wild, the wind in his face;
In graceful movement each step abounds.
Majesty of breed knows no disgrace.
The love for life each day in him resounds.

In captivity, beauty will stand;
Love and loyalty is everywhere
With intelligence to understand.
Through a busy day, there's time to spare.

His mind is sharp, awareness of sense
Keeping his strong head held high and proud.
His wisdom bears truth to common sense.
Regal ways show, speaking clear and loud.

My World of Silence

I feel laughter as I enter the room
For in my world there is silence, not gloom.
I see the happiness in conversations;
There is humanness in situations.

I silently capture and hold what's dear,
But from muffled silence, I have no fear.
Because I'm encouraged to feel and see,
I quickly learn acceptance and feel free.

Pure Confidence

If confidence was all self-made
Then mushrooms would not thrive in shade.
The earthworms would be
A cousin to me,
And we'd dig with a spoon, not a spade.

Optimist's Prayer

An optimist's prayer
Is that he'll be delivered
From the pessimist.

A Mother's Prayer

Shine on, my little star,
My life and small bright light
To become who you are
And to do what is right.

You make a mother proud
For all you are and do;
I'd like to say it loud
How much God's given you.

I pray that you keep strong
In health, in faith, and love,
Throughout a life that's long,
With wisdom from above.

Answers

Answers will be given
to questions that are
asked within proper time.

Casting Stones

Casting stones into
The pond brings stillness to life
The ripples extend.

Life's Easy Breath

Life draws an easy
Breath to make the clear crisp
Sounds for shouts of joy.

History

History's made by all each day;
Each one in their own special way,
Contributing to rise and fall;
Each person here affects us all.
Teachers, merchants, to name a few,
Have much to give both me and you.
If accepted, both bad and good,
History would change, for mankind would.

A Prayer in Memory

He could not find the word
  To express what he felt in pain
In his shattered mind he heard
  her voice in memory plain.

"I love you, Honey; I'll be back soon,"
  And smiled as she closed the door.
Later as he saw the new moon
  A knock came at the door.

Forever the words he will hear:
  The officer's face he'll see.
The love and life he held so dear
  Lies 'neath the old oak tree.

On bended knee each night he falls
  To ask God's loving care.
"Help me, Lord, break down the walls
  That spring up everywhere.

"Help me, dear Lord, to truly live;
  Keep her by Your precious side.
Strengthen me so I may give,
  And ever with You reside."

Let Me Be

I'm one of Mom's children of three
Who just wants to be little me.
I like to read books
And sit in the nooks.
I wish they would just let me be.

Gentle Rain

Gentle rain upon
My windows brings signs of
Life ahead for all.

Togetherness

Whenever it's needed,
Togetherness can be
Comfort to all involved.
For unity to work,
Each must work together.
In times of sorrow,
Quietude, truth, and love
Can be then seen and shown.
If not, in division
All can be destroyed and
In less than a moment,
Only ruins will stand.

The Tree

Stretch out your strong arms
To engulf the life within,
Keeping safe from harms
As life starts therein.

The aged you give rest
From foe's hungry sight,
And cradle small nests
With impressive might.

Standing firm you stay
With proud dignity
With care, guide the way,
True friend ever be.

My Dream

I dream of a world filled with peace
Where wars were ended, hatred ceased.
Clouded shadows have disappeared;
Simple friendships and trust appeared.

Neighbors'll have no quarrels or spats.
Strangers will pass without that
Kind of distance that builds the walls.
There's freedom from divided stalls.

Young and old can walk about free;
Personal storms won't disrupt the sea.
Unity can then be the norm,
No discontent in any form.

Laughter rings out loud and true;
There's contentment for me and you.

Claws

A kitten scratches, but cats claw;
They scrape the surface to find the flaw.
We cook our food while beasts feast raw.
Around the steel, you'll find the straw.

The weather gets cold, yet do we all;
Just turn your back and feel the call.
Outward shall turn to simple withdrawal;
Keep an eye on the hawk, which sees it all.

Talons extend to grasp the bait;
Patience wears thin each time they wait.
Turn and run, but watch the gate—
Fly or stalk, shall seal the fate.

Keep watchful eye and look around
For time will tell the fault that's found.
Then will be no laughter, but the sound
Of claws and teeth, their prey's been found.

Consequence

One old teacher told him he can do
Anything that he set his mind to.
He said with a smirk,
"I won't do the work."
He received both swat one and swat two.

Deciding to Dream

In deciding to
Dream, I either have to wake
Up, or reach for it.

Pride in America

It's been said by Americans everywhere
Through the laughter, the cries, and a loving stare;
It's been stated aloud and in silent word.
The right and love of freedom here can be heard.

We have been through wars, and we have been through
peace;
Each hard time we've known has brought our strength's
increase.
A new light shines through cracks of cold darkness there
In spite of prejudice, we have learned to care.

We carry our heritage with inborn pride
In God and Country, our loyalties reside.
We'll wave our standard high, loudly praises sing;
Honor and duty served, let the anthems ring.

Together As One

The wind rushes all around me.
The breeze cools off the arid warmth.
The time is right to be alive
To walk our paths, to feel, to see.

Voices raise to sing the new day.
Rinse clean within the fresh, clear stream.
Breathe the crisp air of this great land;
Feel the wind as we start our day.

We walk every day together
Talking over sorrows and joys.
United we live, we laugh, and cry—
Life as one we live forever.

Joined, yet separate we will learn
Continued lessons taught by time.
Together we give support;
Bonds of strength and love doesn't burn.

We breathe the breath of new life here;
We trod on this beautiful land.
We watch our days begin and end;
We each feel the breeze, clean and clear.

Feel the gentle wind and stand tall
The brisk breeze can never destroy.
Our time is here to be alive
Together as one, we'll not fall.

Truth's Change

In silence I saw him standing there
As he looked to the hills of his youth.
In hushed retreat he's transported there
To seek some unseen memoric truth.

A soft light crept into his brown eyes;
The square shoulders no longer round.
A hope shone through where answer lies
From a scene far off in sight and sound.

Storm's Strength

The hardships of each
Storm in time will bring droplets
Of strength for new life.

White Squalls

A white screen of flakes
Shoved by wind, forms angry squalls.
They come late this year.

Going Home

My world is crumbling beneath my feet.
The band is playing, but I can't feel the beat.
A world of confusion turns my days into night;
There's a stillness coming over me;
      The candle's no longer bright.

I see in the distance shadows coming near;
The sound of the Angels' wings are ringing in my ear.
They stand in love before me and I know
From family and friends,
      It's time to go.

I turn for one last look and I clearly see
I've done all I could and have been all I could be.
There's no regrets for I know that I have tried.
I've worked and enjoyed;
      I've laughed and I've cried.

The door opens and God asks I enter in
To a bright new world that I will share with Him.
A feeling of peace comes over me I've not known.
I understand now that
      My Father calls me home.